Research on the

OCEANS

ANGELA ROYSTON

First published in 2015 by Wayland

Dewey Number: 551.4'6-dc23.
ISBN: 978 0 7502 8975 7
Library eBook ISBN: 978 0 7502 8018 1
10 9 8 7 6 5 4 3 2 1

MIX
Paper from responsible sources
FSC® C104740

Produced for Wayland by Calcium
Design concept and cover design by Lisa Peacock
Page layout by Keith Williams

Wayland is an imrpint of Hachette Children's Group
Part of Hodder & Stoughton
Carmelite House
50 Victoria Embankment
London EC4Y 0DZ

Picture acknowledgements
Cover: National Oceanic and Atmospheric Administration, Nuytco Research Limited main; Shutterstock: Ase top; Inside: Aquarius Reef Base at Florida International University: 15t, 15b, 17; CAICE, Scripps Institution of Oceanography: M. Dale Stokes 20b; Dreamstime: Aviahuismanphotography 24, Wisconsinart 22; Institute of Marine Research: Kjartan Maestad 10b; Kraft TeleRobotics Inc.: 10t; NASA: 14, 16t; National Oceanic and Atmospheric Administration: 6l, 12, 26, 12–13, Life on the Edge 2004 Expedition: NOAA Office of Ocean Exploration 6r, MARUM, University of Bremen and NOAA-Pacific Marine Environmental Laboratory 7, OAR/National Undersea Research Program 5, 16b, NOAA Okeanos Explorer Program 25, 27, 28t, Pacific Islands Fisheries Science Center 29; Shutterstock: Ethan Daniels 28b, Levent Konuk 19b, Lebendkulturen.de 20t, Michal Ninger 23b, Shin Okamoto 18, Khoroshunova Olga 1, 4t, 8, Alexius Sutandio 19t; Wikimedia Commons: Gleam 23t, Mike 9, NOAA 4b, Saoysters 21; Chris Griner/Woods Hole Oceanographic Institution: 11.

Printed in China

An Hachette UK company
www.hachette.co.uk
www.hachettechildrens.co.uk

CONTENTS

SCIENCE IN THE DEEP

The oceans cover nearly three-quarters of Earth's surface, and in places they are deeper than the highest mountains. Below the surface of the sea is an amazing underwater world inhabited by shoals of fish and other sea creatures. Farther from shore, the seabed drops away to the deep ocean. Here mountains and volcanoes rise from the ocean floor and canyons form deep trenches. In some places, hot water gushes from cracks called hydrothermal vents.

Divers use equipment such as aqualungs to examine sea life on the seabed.

A hydrothermal vent is a crack in the ocean floor where hot water escapes from deep inside Earth.

Ocean Lessons

Studying the oceans provides vital information about our planet, from the destructive effects of global warming to the prediction of undersea earthquakes that can cause tsunamis (see page 22). The discovery of new species can lead to the development of better medicines, and increases our understanding of evolution and adaptation. There is still much to find out – scientists at the US government agency NOAA (National Oceanic and Atmospheric Administration) estimate that 95 per cent of the world's oceans remain unexplored.

This scientist is so deep below the ocean's surface that he is using a submersible with lights to study the seafloor.

Dangerous Work

Aquanauts work on the edge, facing hazards and challenges as they research sea life and explore the ocean floor. Some dive down to the seabed to gather material. Others spend months at sea. Marine scientists rely on a wide range of specialized equipment, including aqualungs and undersea cameras. The latest technology includes robots and remotely controlled vehicles, such as ISIS. This book looks at how marine scientists carry out their work, who funds this research and at some of the results.

CUTTING EDGE

ISIS is a state-of-the-art submersible that works in deep water and treacherous conditions. A submersible is a small underwater vehicle that is supported by a shore team, a larger submarine or in the case of ISIS, by a ship on the surface. ISIS has been in action at undersea volcanoes in the Caribbean and at the bottom of a 5-kilometre (3-mile) deep canyon off the coast of Portugal. It is equipped with high-definition video cameras, chemical sensors and manipulator arms for collecting samples.

SAVING THE OCEANS

Researching the oceans has never been more important because they are under threat as never before. Pollution poisons the water and huge fishing trawlers rake vast areas of seabed. The trawlers destroy seabed environments and leave once-thriving fishing grounds barren. Overfishing, when more fish are taken from the sea than can be replaced by the remaining fish, is a constant problem. Coral reefs are rich in fishes and all types of marine life, but warming seas and overfishing are damaging them.

Working Against Time

Scientists need to work fast to study and record all the different ocean habitats and millions of species before many are lost for ever. Scientists also monitor and measure what is happening to the oceans and their wildlife. They then publish this research to raise awareness of the plight of the oceans.

Scientists are interested in deep-sea coral and the fishes that live around them.

This giant mechanical claw carefully lifts a sample of rock from the seafloor.

A suction tube collects a sample without disturbing anything around it.

Working Carefully

Scientists know that what happens in one place or to one species can affect other habitats and other species. As they carry out their research, they try to disturb the habitat as little as possible and to do no harm. For example, they may have to collect samples from the seabed. Instead of using a rake like a fishing trawler, they use a suction trawler, which gently sucks up specific samples. The device is operated remotely and has a small video camera to show the scientist what is happening.

CUTTING EDGE

Creatures who live at the bottom of the oceans live in total darkness, so scientists have to photograph and film them without using bright lights. To do this, they use LED lights and cameras that operate in low light. LED lamps give a red light, which does not disturb deep-sea fishes, but is picked up by the cameras.

UNDERWATER EXPLORATION

Scuba divers can navigate marine structures such as coral reefs near the ocean surface.

Working at or under the sea can be difficult and dangerous. To study marine life up close, researchers dive below the ocean's surface. The sea, however, becomes colder and darker as the depth increases. The Sun's warmth and light reach only about 200 metres (656 feet) below the surface. Even this depth is beyond the reach of divers.

Diving Gear

The ocean is a hostile environment for humans. Divers need special equipment to breathe underwater, flippers to help them move and masks to allow them to see clearly. They have to handle sea creatures carefully to avoid being stung by jellyfish and other species. Diving suits keep scientists warm in the ocean and help to protect them from painful jellyfish stings. Scuba divers carry a cylinder with a supply of gas to breathe. For deeper or longer dives, marine scientists are supplied with breathing gas through a pipe from a ship on the surface.

These divers are using oxygen cylinders to provide them with gas to breathe.

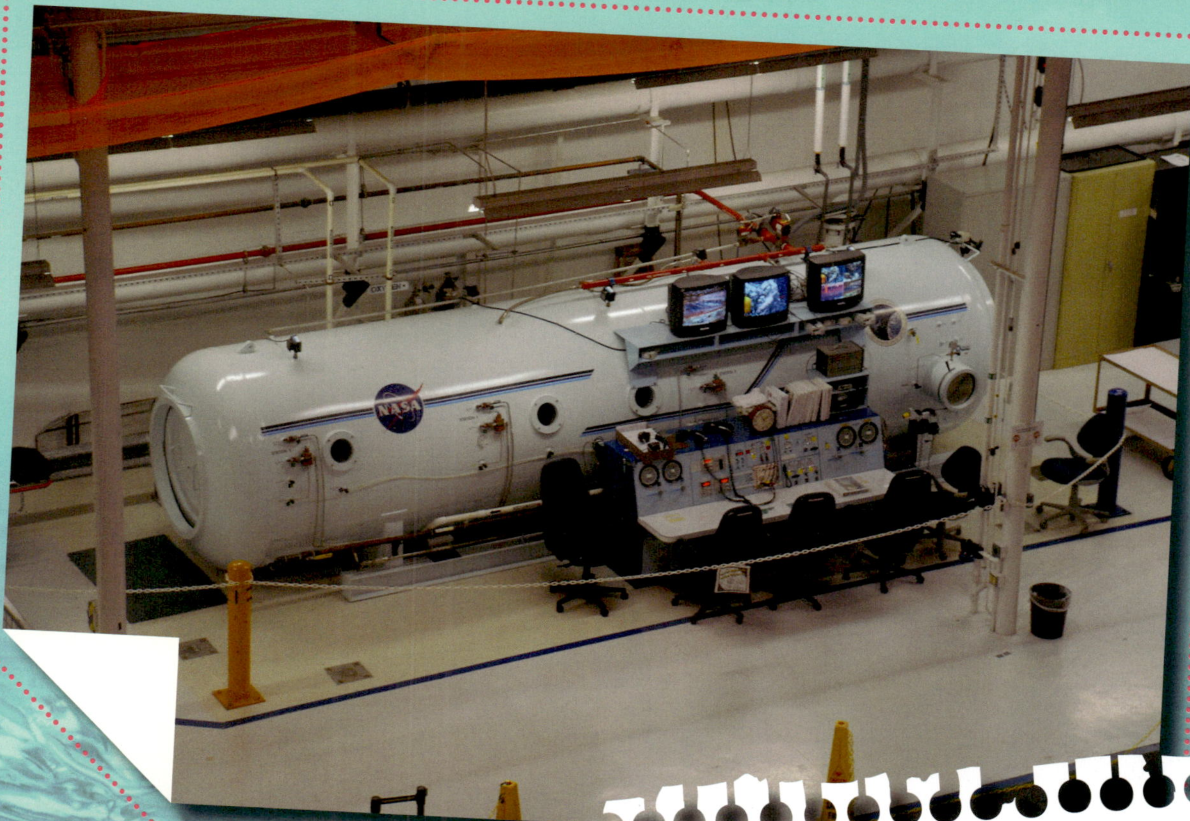

This decompression chamber holds several people at once. Pressure inside the chamber is monitored and controlled by those outside.

Under Pressure

The biggest problem for divers is water pressure produced by the weight of seawater above them. In the deepest parts of the ocean, nearly 11 kilometres (6.8 miles) below the surface, water pressure is equivalent to a person being crushed under the weight of 50 jumbo jets! Scientists, however, do not dive deeper than 145 metres (476 feet) below the surface. To study the ocean floor, they use other means.

DANGER!

Decompression sickness, also called 'the bends', is a major hazard for divers. When water pressure increases, nitrogen dissolves in a diver's blood. As the diver returns to the surface, the pressure reduces and bubbles of the gas form in the diver's body. This is very painful and can be lethal. To avoid the bends, divers decompress very slowly. They spend hours in a special chamber, where the pressure is slowly decreased. The deeper and longer the dive, the longer it takes divers to decompress.

SCIENCE ON THE MOVE

This remotely controlled vehicle, *Hercules*, is carrying out an experiment on the seafloor.

To travel around and study the oceans, scientists use special boats, or research vessels (RVs). Most sea life is found in shallow waters near the coast, and so a small boat can usually take scientists to the site of their research. Much larger RVs are used to go farther afield and to study the deep ocean.

The Norwegian ship *G.O. Sars* is a state-of-the-art RV. Its engines are much quieter than other ships so they do not disturb the sea life being studied.

Ocean-Going RVs

The largest RVs are longer than a football pitch. They can stay at sea for several months and carry teams of scientists to study different aspects of an area. The team might include marine biologists, geologists and oceanographers. The ship has equipment on board for trawling the seabed, sampling the water and tracking fish and other sea creatures. It also includes a laboratory so that samples can be analyzed on the spot.

Nereus is lowered into the sea off the Massachusetts coast in the USA.

Robot Research

To reach great depths, scientists use submersibles and robots. Most submersibles are unmanned and are either controlled from a ship or are pre-programmed to work autonomously. Submersibles carry lights, cameras and special tools for collecting samples.

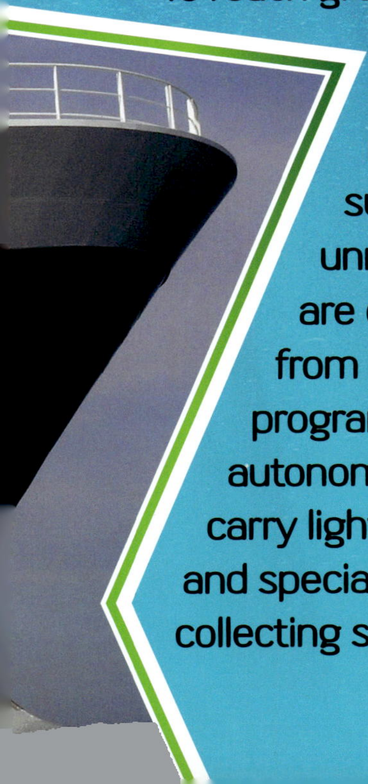

CUTTING EDGE

Nereus is an unmanned submersible that is owned by the Woods Hole Oceanographic Institution in the United States. It can be controlled from a ship through a 40-kilometre- (25-mile-) long cable, or it can operate as an autonomous underwater vehicle (AUV). *Nereus* made the deepest unmanned submersible dive ever when it descended 10.9 kilometres (6.8 miles) to the bottom of the Marianas ocean trench.

AQUARIUS – OCEAN LAB

Aquarius is an underwater laboratory situated 5.6 kilometres (3.5 miles) off the coast of Florida, USA. It gives scientists a unique, cutting-edge opportunity to live and work underwater for days or weeks at a time.

Saturation Diving

Most divers can stay underwater only for a few hours before they have to return to the surface and decompress. Researchers on Aquarius, however, use a technique called saturation diving.

A diver can use frames to measure the size of specimens on the seabed.

This technique allows divers' blood to become saturated with nitrogen, the gas that causes decompression sickness (see page 9). Once their blood is saturated, it will absorb no more nitrogen and divers can stay underwater, living and working in Aquarius for as long as they like. Most missions last about ten days, during which scientists spend up to nine hours a day in the water. In this time they can achieve results that would normally take ten weeks.

Aquarius is the world's only underwater laboratory for marine scientists.

Underwater Structure

Aquarius is built in shallow water on the ocean floor just 18 metres (59 feet) below the surface of the sea. It is fixed to a strong, heavy baseplate that keeps it firmly in place on the ocean floor. The laboratory is about 13 metres (43 feet) long and 3 metres (9 feet) wide. As well as a working area with computers and equipment, Aquarius includes living space with six bunk beds.

DANGER!

Hurricanes and severe storms frequently hit the coast of Florida. Both the baseplate and the lab have been designed to withstand extreme weather. Nevertheless, when a hurricane is predicted, the aquanauts are evacuated to dry land. The decision to evacuate has to be made well before the hurricane strikes to give the aquanauts time to decompress inside Aquarius.

MISSION CONTROL

Scientists on Aquarius are in constant contact with colleagues on the surface. These scientists work in a structure called the Life Support Buoy. The circular buoy is 10 metres (33 feet) in diameter and is tethered in position above Aquarius. A 7-centimetre (3-inch) wide tube links the buoy with the lab and supplies the aquanauts with air and oxygen, as well as electricity cables.

The crew of Aquarius is made up of four scientists and two technicians (pictured inside Aquarius).

Communication Made Simple

The Life Support Buoy is a communication centre between the lab and Mission Control in Key Largo 12 kilometres (7.5 miles) away. Mission Control is in charge of the whole operation and is also linked to Aquarius by wireless telemetry, a system that uses radio waves to send data. Controllers keep aquanauts informed about the weather and monitor conditions inside Aquarius. A decompression chamber, which can be used to evacuate an aquanaut in a hurry, is kept at Mission Control.

CUTTING EDGE

Aquarius is used not only by marine scientists but also by the National Aeronautics and Space Administration (NASA). NASA uses it to train astronauts, engineers and scientists for long space missions. Astronauts spend up to three weeks at a time in Aquarius. Here they face the challenges of living in an extreme environment, and venture outside the lab for the deep-sea equivalent of 'space walks'.

Getting to Aquarius

Divers use scuba equipment to reach the lab from a small boat on the surface. They then go through the entry lock into a 'wet porch', which is closed off from the rest of Aquarius. The wet porch has a dry area with air, and a moon pool with the entrance to the sea at the bottom. Once they are under the sea, scientists can travel to and from Aquarius to study marine life.

The Life Support Buoy floats on the surface above Aquarius.

Divers prepare on a support boat on the surface of the ocean before diving down to the laboratory below.

LIFE IN THE LAB

Aquarius is no bigger than a train carriage but it contains everything four scientists and two technicians need to live and to work under the sea. As well as computers and equipment, it has a kitchen area, shower, toilet and six bunk beds. Once aquanauts have unpacked their own equipment and personal belongings, there is hardly room to move! Aquanauts sleep in two stacks of narrow bunks, one above the other.

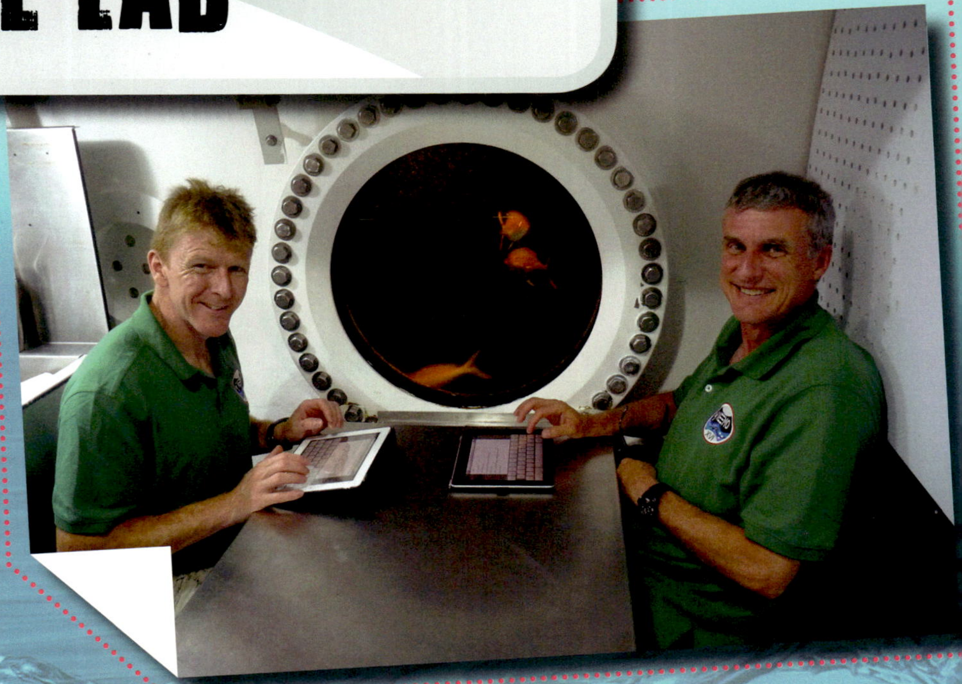

There is little time off under the sea! Scientists have to type up the results of their research to send back to Mission Control.

A Working Day

Aquarius is situated close to coral reefs and that is where the scientists spend most of their working day. Among other projects, their work includes monitoring the effect of climate change on the reef.

A talk bubble allows divers to communicate outside Aquarius. The round dome contains a bubble of air in which divers can breathe and talk to each other.

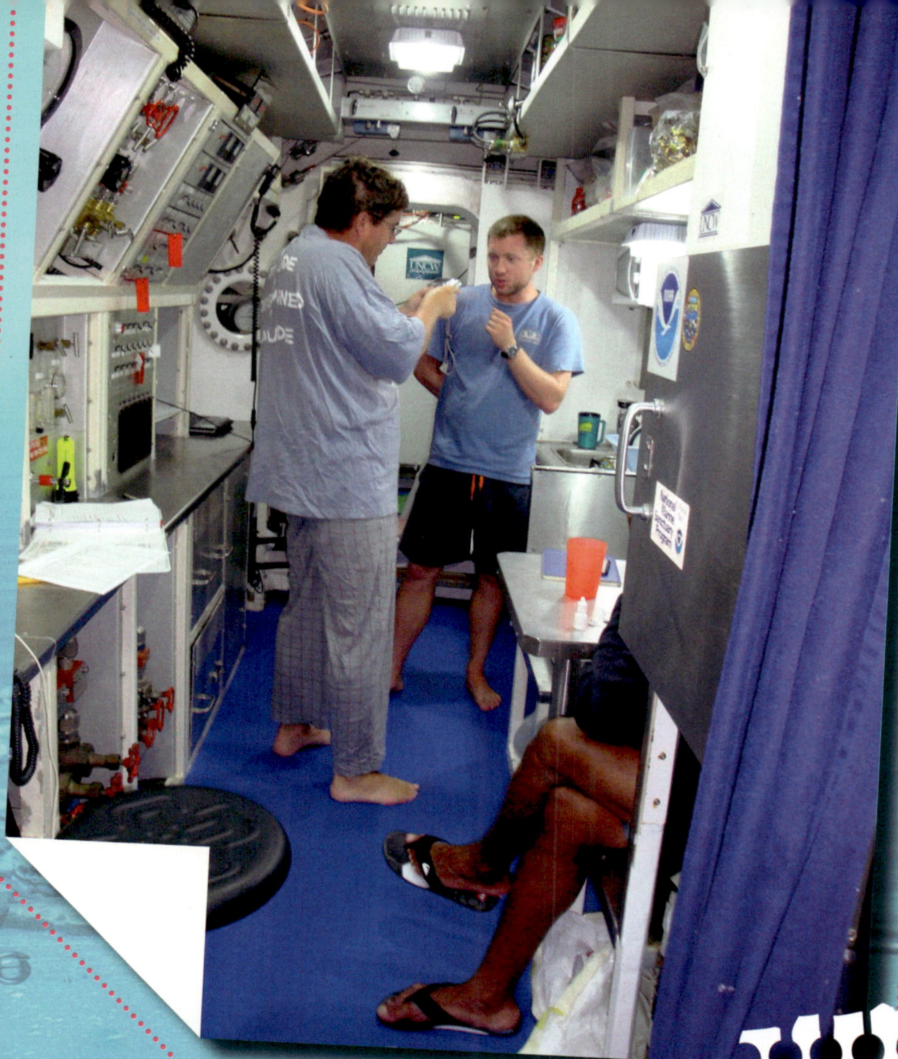

The kitchen area in Aquarius includes pressure taps and other equipment – every bit of space is used!

On the Surface

At the end of a mission, aquanauts decompress for about 17 hours inside Aquarius. The pressure is slowly reduced until it is the same as that on the surface. Then the aquanauts leave the lab through the moon pool and swim to the surface. Onshore they are monitored for 12 hours to make sure they have not suffered any ill effects from decompression.

Scientists also spend time studying sea creatures and how they help to keep the balance of the ocean, for example, they have discovered that sea sponges help to clean the water around the reefs. Back in the lab, scientists may carry out experiments before uploading their data to send to Mission Control.

DANGER!

In case of emergencies, Aquarius's designers provided a safe shelter, called the Gazebo, alongside the wet porch. The Gazebo is big enough to hold six people standing up. The air is ventilated from a store of high-pressure air on the baseplate, so aquanauts can survive there until they are rescued.

MYSTERIES OF THE DEEP

Scientists working on Aquarius, and at other ocean labs all around the world, are constantly on the lookout for new species. In the first decade of the twenty-first century, nearly 3,000 marine biologists worked together to take the Census of Marine Life. They searched the deepest and the coldest seas as well as coastal habitats looking for and counting every type of living organism, from microscopic plankton to the blue whale. In the process they discovered more than 6,000 new marine species, as well as 17,000 different species on the ocean bed.

Abundant Bacteria

The oceans swarm with bacteria. The Census of Marine Life found that 1 litre (0.2 gallons) of seawater contains 38,000 different species of microbe. Most of these are essential to many food chains. For example, scientists found that in hydrothermal vents, bacteria thrive on chemicals in the gases and rocks. In turn, giant tubeworms survive by consuming the bacteria.

It is difficult to study animals that are constantly on the move. The Census tagged and tracked large animals such as sea lions.

Crabs and Sea Stars

Scientists are finding strange new sea creatures almost everywhere, particularly on the ocean floor. For example, a crab with no eyes was found on a hydrothermal vent in the Pacific Ocean and a bright purple sea star was found on a coral reef.

Using satellites to keep track of tagged great white sharks, scientists have discovered that these fearsome creatures often migrate across the ocean.

This diver is exploring the marine life, around an area of soft coral.

CUTTING EDGE

Scientists working on the Census invented new ways of taking samples of marine life. The Autonomous Reef Monitoring Structure (ARMS) was created to sample life on a coral reef in Indonesia and is now used at reefs around the world. It consists of a box with several plastic plates that is left in the water for a year. Species use the box like an artificial reef, making them easy to study when the box is retrieved.

WHAT'S DOWN THERE?

As scientists explore the oceans, it is becoming increasingly clear how climate change is affecting the ocean environment. Research is showing that both carbon dioxide levels and water temperatures are rising in oceans around the world. These discoveries confirm that the effects of climate change are occurring much faster than predicted, putting pressure on governments and people to work together.

This tiny shrimp is just one of many types of crustacean found in plankton. These organisms are being severely affected by climate change.

This experiment to investigate the effect of waves breaking on a beach is being carried out in the controlled conditions of a laboratory.

Acid Ocean

Carbon dioxide combines with seawater to produce carbonic acid, just as it combines with rainwater to produce acid rain. The acid makes it harder for crustaceans to build their shells. This affects young crabs, shrimps, squid and other shellfish. The tiny polyps that build coral reefs are already taking longer to build their reefs. Plankton includes many tiny crustaceans, such as copepods. Scientists have found that, as the sea becomes more acidic, plankton is decreasing. This will have a knock-on affect on ocean food chains.

CUTTING EDGE

A new area of research is to study climate change by using satellite images of plankton as well as by taking seawater samples. Although plankton is invisible to the naked eye, large amounts of it show up on satellite photos. The satellite images show what happens to plankton in different parts of the ocean at different times of the year.

Hot, Hot, Hotter

Research has also shown that ocean temperatures are rising around the world. This is worrying for two reasons: the rise in temperature risks damaging the fragile ecosystems under the sea; and as water heats up, it expands. This means that sea levels are rising, threatening low-lying and coastal communities around the world.

An oyster farm raises tonnes of oysters for people to eat. As the sea becomes acidic, however, life is becoming more difficult for the oysters and their farmers.

AT THE BOTTOM OF THE SEA

Marine geologists carry out research on rocks and sediments on the seafloor and on the landscapes of the seabed, such as undersea mountains, deep chasms, wide plains and long mountain ridges. They study how new ocean floor is produced by undersea volcanoes, and how earthquakes cause tsunamis.

This artist's picture captures the terrifying force of a tsunami hitting the coast.

Tsunami Surges

A tsunami is a series of huge waves that rolls across the ocean and sweeps over the land, drowning people and destroying buildings, trees and crops. A tsunami may be triggered by an earthquake in the seafloor, or by a massive chunk of land sliding into the sea.

Undersea Tremors

Scientists use seismometers to study underwater Earth movements. Some seismometers are set up around hot spots and then collected after a period of time so that their data can be studied. Others are linked to early-warning centres, to help scientists predict when a tsunami is likely to occur and to warn people to evacuate coastal areas.

Drilling on the ocean floor can uncover evidence of prehistoric life, such as this fossil of a trilobite.

Drilling

Scientists study the ocean floor to learn about the past as well as the future. They use ships equipped with massive drills to bore into the seabed and extract long cores of sediment and rocks. They then examine the cores to find out what the oceans and climate were like in the past and to look for early forms of life.

The drillship *Chikyu* can drill in water up to 2 kilometres (6,500 feet) deep. One day it may even drill right through Earth's crust into the mantle!

CUTTING EDGE

The Japanese drillship *Chikyu* can bore up to 7,000 metres (23,000 feet) into the seabed, deeper than any other ship. It is designed to operate in earthquake zones. Scientists hope that it will help them to understand and predict tsunamis.

FUNDING RESEARCH

Researching the oceans costs a huge amount of money. Universities and governments fund most research, but companies are keen to be involved in research that leads to new materials or medicines from which they can make billions of dollars. For example, oil companies fund geological research to identify new oil reserves under the ocean bed. Pharmaceutical companies buy the rights to develop medicines from marine species by helping to fund the research.

Sharing Costs

The costs of large projects are shared by many organizations. The Census of Marine Life, which involved 2,700 scientists and cost US$650 million, received funds from 2,000 different groups and involved 80 countries. The Japanese drillship *Chikyu* is part of an international research project called the Integrated Ocean Drilling Program. Scientists and drillships from many countries work together, sharing the costs and the results.

Medicines From the Oceans

Sharing costs makes large projects possible and is particularly useful when the research is available to everyone. What is more contentious is when companies claim the exclusive rights to develop products from particular research. For example, Oceanyx, a drug development company, bought the exclusive rights to marine research from a lab at the University of Florida. This means that no other institution or company can use this research.

CUTTING EDGE

Oceanyx is using marine research to produce new drugs. It is investigating the marine microbes in seawater and from sediments on the ocean floor. It has found two substances, largazole and apratoxin, which it hopes will become important drugs in the treatment of cancer and bone diseases.

This RV is owned by NOAA. Scientists onboard are investigating the impact of oil in the Gulf of Mexico after an oil spill in 2010.

NOAA's latest technology allows video and data collected by a submersible to be transmitted to a research ship, from where it is beamed live by satellite to scientists on the shore.

SHARING SCIENCE

The results of marine researchers' experiments can impact us all. Over the past decades, marine research has led to developments in medicine, awareness of the destruction caused by overfishing and fish farming, and a realization that the effects of climate change are happening faster than anticipated. But how are the results of research made public?

Marine scientists sort and label specimens on which their research is based. Once their research is complete, it is made public.

Publishing a Paper

Once scientists have obtained their results, they publish them in scientific journals. Before a paper is published, the journal sends it to other scientists who are experts in the fields. These experts make sure that the methods used are reliable and that the data supports the conclusions. Other scientists and experts keep themselves informed by reading the journals.

Using Research

Published research gives governments and other groups reliable information on which to make decisions or press for change. For example, scientists have shown how factory fishing destroys the whole undersea environment, making it difficult for sea life to recover. They have also shown that if fishing is strictly controlled or banned before the area is destroyed, sea life thrives and actually repopulates the water outside the reserve.

CUTTING EDGE

A scientific paper can encourage further research. For example, in 2002 a new species of worm was discovered. These worms fed on the skeletons of fishes and whales on the seabed. The scientists called them zombie worms, but they could not work out how the worms ate when they had no mouth or gut. In 2012 a different group of scientists found the answer. The worms attached themselves to the skeleton bones with 'roots' that produce acid. The acid bores into the bones and allows the worms to extract the nutrients within the bones.

Research institutes share photos, such as this image of an ocean eel, and information with the general public as well as with other scientists.

SAVE OUR SEAS

As well as exploring the unknown, scientists monitor changes and warn about problems for the future. The most critical problems affecting the oceans are overfishing and climate change. In the tropics, many coral reefs are dying as coral polyps cannot survive in the increasingly warm seas.

NOAA's ship *Okeanos Explorer* can carry 25 people, including the crew, scientists and sometimes a school teacher or students. The ship is used to explore unknown ocean to advance people's knowledge of the seas.

Parts of this yellow coral reef have become bleached because the seawater has become too warm for the coral polyps to survive.

Protecting Sea Life

Conservation charities around the world raise money to protect ocean species and habitats. They use scientific research to publicize the problems and to persuade governments to introduce laws to combat them. In the past, many species of whale nearly became extinct, so a ban on whaling was introduced to save the whales. Now sharks are threatened as large numbers are killed to provide fins for shark-fin soup. Scientists are trying to persuade the United Nations to ban shark hunting.

A marine reserve can be created in coastal waters as well as farther out to sea.

Marine Reserves

Scientists want to go much further than protecting a few particular species. They argue that large areas of the ocean should become marine reserves, where fishing is strictly controlled and the entire environment is protected. This would stop oil and mining companies from damaging seabed habitats in these areas. Where small marine reserves have been set up, the fish stocks and seabed habitats are recovering.

CUTTING EDGE

Research in the oceans is helping scientists look for alien life forms in space. Species have been found living in extreme environments, which scientists previously thought were too hostile for life. These environments include hydrothermal vents, extremely cold seas under the Antarctic and places without oxygen. Scientists are now looking for similar forms of life on planets and icy moons that were previously considered uninhabitable.

GLOSSARY

aqualung A device, which includes a tank of compressed air, that divers use to breathe under water.

aquanaut A person who lives in an underwater habitat.

autonomously Independently.

breathing gas A mixture of gases that includes oxygen and is suitable for humans to breathe.

climate change Changes in climate around the world caused by an increase in carbon dioxide and other gases in the atmosphere. Climate change causes warming seas, melting polar ice and extreme weather.

decompress To reduce pressure inside the body or on an object.

decompression sickness A serious and painful condition caused when bubbles of nitrogen form in the blood and joints. It occurs when divers decompress too quickly.

evacuated Ordered to leave a dangerous place or area.

geologist A scientist who studies the rocks and solid Earth.

manipulator arm A device that is remotely controlled to pick up or move things.

mantle The layer of hot, molten rock that lies under Earth's solid outer crust.

marine biologist A scientist who studies animals, plants and other forms of life in the sea.

marine scientist A scientist who studies the seas and oceans.

monitor To observe and record.

moon pool A pool that divers can use to gain access to and from the sea through an entrance at the bottom.

oceanographer A scientist who studies everything to do with the oceans, including the seawater, currents, waves and marine life.

organism A form of life.

plankton Microscopic plants and animals that float near the surface of the water and provide food for sea animals.

remotely controlled vehicle A vehicle that is controlled through an electric cable or wireless connection by an operator who is not onboard.

research vessel A boat or ship that is equipped with everything scientists need to research the oceans.

saturated Unable to absorb any more of a substance.

saturation diving When a diver's body becomes saturated with nitrogen. This allows the diver to stay underwater for long periods of time without further increasing the time needed to decompress.

seismometer An instrument that measures vibrations in the ground.

submersible A small submarine.

tethered Connected.

unmanned Without a crew.

water pressure The force produced by a mass of water.

wireless telemetry Radio signals used to monitor the environment.

ventilated Kept supplied with fresh air.

FURTHER READING

Books

Habitat Survival: Oceans.
Claire Llewellyn, Raintree, 2013.

Illustrated Enclyclopedia of the Ocean.
Dorling Kindersley, 2011.

Saving Wildlife: Ocean Animals.
Sonya Newland, Franklin Watts, 2011.

Unstable Earth: What Happens if We Overfish the Oceans? Angela Royston, Wayland, 2013.

What's It Like to Be a Marine Biologist?
Elizabeth Dowen, A&C Black, 2010.

Websites

Find out about coral reefs at this website designed for children:
http://kids.nceas.ucsb.edu/biomes/coralreef.html

Explore National Geographic's website on the oceans to find out about ocean life, underwater exploration and how to protect the ocean at:
http://ocean.nationalgeographic.com/ocean

This page on the NOAA website leads to information about diving and Aquarius Underwater Laboratory:
http://oceanexplorer.noaa.gov/technology/diving/diving.html

Find out all about the deep sea, including the Census of Marine Life, ocean drilling and other technology at:
http://ocean.si.edu/deep-sea

The video *Acid Test: The Global Challenge of Ocean Acidification*, shows you some of the amazing diversity of life and how it is threatened by acidity due to increased carbon dioxide.
You can see it at:
www.youtube.com/watch?v=5cqCvcX7buo

INDEX